Through the Fire

---•---

By Tricia Jordan

Through the Fire

Trilogy Christian Publishers A Wholly Owned Subsidiary of Trinity Broadcasting Network

2442 Michelle Drive Tustin, CA 92780

Copyright © 2023 by Tricia Jordan

Unless otherwise noted, all Scripture quotations are taken from the ESV® Bible (The Holy Bible, English Standard Version®), copyright © 2001 by Crossway Bibles, a publishing ministry of Good News Publishers. Used by permission. All rights reserved. Scripture quotations marked NIV are taken from the Holy Bible, New International Version®, NIV®. Copyright © 1973, 1978, 1984, 2011 by Biblica, Inc.TM Used by permission of Zondervan. All rights reserved worldwide. www.zondervan.com. The "NIV" and "New International Version" are trademarks registered in the United States Patent and Trademark Office by Biblica, Inc.™

No part of this book may be reproduced, stored in a retrieval system, or transmitted by any means without written permission from the author. All rights reserved. Printed in the USA.

Rights Department, 2442 Michelle Drive, Tustin, CA 92780.

Trilogy Christian Publishing/TBN and colophon are trademarks of Trinity Broadcasting Network.

Cover design by Kate Kohn

For information about special discounts for bulk purchases, please contact Trilogy Christian Publishing.

Trilogy Disclaimer: The views and content expressed in this book are those of the author and may not necessarily reflect the views and doctrine of Trilogy Christian Publishing or the Trinity Broadcasting Network. In the book, some of the names have been changed to protect identities.

Manufactured in the United States of America

10 9 8 7 6 5 4 3 2 1

Library of Congress Cataloging-in-Publication Data is available.

ISBN: 979-8-88738-908-0

E-ISBN: 979-8-88738-909-7

Tricia,

Through all of your trials, you have remained my spiritual advisor, shown me the true Word and how He truly feels for His children and how to walk in His light, the power of prayer, how to recognize His Spirit interacting with mine versus the belief that it's my intuition, sharing the love and wonder gifted to us by Jesus Christ. I pray to follow your life's walk and lift others around me in the same humble manner.

—Tina Henry

Table of Contents

Foreword	7
Introduction	10
A Little about Me	11
The Fall	17
Oh My God, No!	19
Saying Goodbye Is Hard	25
Dealing with Fear	33
My House Is on Fire	37
The Wreck	43
The Girls	45
My Family	51
My Nephews	55
Some Awesome Miracles	59
The Arrest	63
The Hardest Thing I Have Ever Been Through	73
Knowing God	89

Foreword

For we live by faith, not by sight.

2 Corinthians 5:7 (NIV)

Patricia Jordan was sent to me by Jesus. I just did not know it at the time. I was six years old when I decided that I wanted to be a lawyer. That was a choice that was made (at first) based upon immature insight. But, by the time I was sitting inside a law school classroom, the goal of becoming an attorney was almost insight and felt destined. After what seemed like an endurance test, law school was complete, and my bar exam was over, and then I waited months for results. I prayed. I bargained with God that if He would let me pass, I would promise to help people. I passed.

My first year of practice was less than glamorous. I am not sure if I really helped anyone during that first year, but I realized that the legal job I had was not satisfying my curiosity or desire to help anyone. Despite spending nine years at that law firm, I knew I needed to move on.

I started working at a criminal defense firm where the owner was an alum of my law school. I hated it the moment I started. I had always pictured myself being a prosecutor, but I remained at the large law firm I worked for prior to law school because they paid much more than the district attorney's office. When I left, I knew I would take a pay cut. And I did. I did not know that the office I would work in would test everything I believed in.

I was just about to quit when I was assigned Patricia's case. I read the notes that the partner had written down about the case. Patricia had traveled to New York with her teenage daughter. Patricia was a legal gun owner in her home state, but she traveled to New York City without having a valid license to have her gun in New York. It was not the most legally complex case. I called Patricia because I was going to work on a mitigation packet, and the minute I heard her voice, I realized she was a different type of client than I was used to working in criminal defense. She was not a rule breaker; she was a mom. A mom who had experienced plenty of trauma and carried a legal weapon for safety. I learned about her family, her marriage, and her daughter. Simply, she was inspiring.

This is her story. This is her journey. This is how Patricia walks by faith and not sight and with Jesus. Her story is one that will make you evaluate your own faith and will renew your belief in the fact we all walk a path we cannot see but that He can. Patricia will detail how we met and how that experience impacted her and her family. What she does not know is that it impacted me.

After Patricia and I completed our phone call, I knew about her and her traumas. What I did not know what that meeting her was the first step of healing my own broken heart. I bargained with God again—I promised Him that if He would help me help Patricia, I would come up with an effective plan to help other people. When we reached a disposition in Patricia's case, I knew I had to pay up. I just was not sure how I would do that. For the first year, I volunteered with underprivileged kids and mentored them about attending college—coaching them in academics and encouraging them to keep trying. Then two years after meeting Patricia, I knew I was on the wrong side of aisle in the criminal justice system. I was a good defense attorney, but every time I helped a client who faced a criminal sex charge, I lost a part of me. So, remembering Patricia's, Terry's, and Carmen's faces when we left the Queens Criminal Court, I knew I could no longer be a defense attorney.

Patricia's journey intersected with my path. Today, I practice law with a soul. She pushed me down my path and closer to God without even realizing it. I now represent survivors of sexual assault. Most of my clients were sexually abused as children. Each day I work with my clients, they heal me. They remind me that faith in God can lead to justice.

—Hillary Nappi

Introduction

My name is Patricia Louise Sanford Jordan; I go by Tricia. I felt like I was supposed to write this book to share my story. I am not a writer, so as you read about everything I have been through in my life, I hope you see my heart and, most importantly, that God has been with me through it all. He has brought me through so much, and on my journey, He has taught me about His grace, compassion, peace, forgiveness, and to totally depend on Him, not just daily but every second of every minute. I am so thankful I had such an awesome mom that loved the Lord and taught me how to depend on Him through everything in my life.

(I realize that my family's memories may be different than mine because I am remembering so much from such a young age, but these are my memories.)

A Little about Me

I was born March 7, 1971, in Rome, Georgia, to Wallace Harold Sanford, Sr, my dad, who was forty-two years old, and Dorothy (Dot) Summey Sanford, my mom, who was forty years old. I was the uh-oh baby. I had four siblings and two nieces when I was born. My oldest brother, Thomas, was twenty and married to Ann. My oldest sister, Linda, was eighteen. She was married and had Tracey, who was two years old, and Tyra, who was three weeks older than me. Yes, my mom and sister were pregnant at the same time with us. Then, my middle sister Lisa was ten, and my youngest brother Kevin was six.

My parents lived at 22 Pine St, in Cartersville, Georgia. It was a cute little house my dad had built in 1954. I lived there with my parents and my two youngest siblings until I was about nine months old, and then we moved to our home at 8 Assembly Dr., which my dad had built in 1972. It was literally a block away from our other home. It was a white brick ranch home on two acres with three bedrooms, two baths, and a full basement with an apartment in it. We always used the carport door to come into our house; no one ever used the front door. When you came into our house from the front door, there was the foyer, and to the right was the formal living room. It had floor-to-ceiling glass windows all the way across the front of the living room. I would love to sit on the couch and watch the snow in front of the windows. At Christmas, my mom always had a 1950s silver tinsel tree with silver silk-like ornaments with a revolving light that had four colors that would shine on the tree. I would sit and watch how the light would change the tree from red, blue, yellow, and green. It's one of my favorite Christmas memories. The living room is also where my mom would pray most of the time. She would get on her face on the floor and lay for hours praying. The dining room wall had a huge mural of a port city. It always made me think of a city in Spain or France that was on a hill looking over the ocean with boats. If you went straight out of the foyer, you ended up in our den, which was large. It had a fireplace on the back wall that took up half of the room, a large window to the left of the fireplace, and a door to the right of the fireplace that went onto the porch. My dad had also put wooden beams on the ceiling. I remember the floor had linoleum that had a pattern on it, and I'd love to get a piece of paper and a pencil and rub the pencil on the paper on the floor so you could see the design on the paper. At Christmas, we had our family Christmas tree in this room in the corner, near the big window by the fireplace. I remember one Christmas walking into the den on Christmas morning, and Santa had left me a huge monkey I had been looking at and carrying around the store with me for a month. He was hanging from the light fixture. I was so excited! He was as big as I was, but his hands and feet had Velcro on them, so he would wrap around you. I used to carry him everywhere with me. To the right of the den were saloon doors (that's what I called them) going into the breakfast room and kitchen. The kitchen was U-shaped with tons of cabinets and counter space.

We had a bar from the breakfast room side that I would sit at and watch my mom make homemade biscuits. Her biscuits were the best. She also made great homemade cornbread and chicken and dumplings; they were my favorite. Our family table was in the breakfast area. It was a wooden clawfoot table. Then from the breakfast area toward the laundry room was the door leading to the carport on the right. This is the door everyone used to come into our home. In the breakfast room were sliding glass doors that led out onto our screened-in back porch. My parents loved to have people over for steak dinners, and my dad would cook for them on our grill that was on the screened porch. It was a built-in grill, not like our portable ones today. Back in the den, going left from the foyer, was the hall that led to the bedrooms. In the first door to the right in the hall were the stairs going to the basement. The next door led to the main bathroom. It had a vanity with a stool and a cool sink, of which the left side was slanted like a slide. I used to play like it was a pool with a slide for my barbie dolls. The bathroom had a door to my parents' master bedroom. Their bedroom was the last door on the right. My dad had put a deck off of the master bedroom. It overlooked an area that was supposed to have a water fountain but never did, so my mom would plant her banana plants there instead. If you knew my mom, you knew she loved her banana plants. On the left side of the hall were my bedroom and my sister Lisa's bedroom, with a bathroom between the two bedrooms. Once my dad finished the basement, half of it was an apartment with a full bath, kitchen, living area, and a bedroom with a walk-in closet. My younger brother Keith lived here when he got older. The rest was just a garage area. It had a circular driveway all the way around the back of the house. At the lower end of the house, my dad had built a building with two car stalls and another area so he could work on cars. He and my younger brother would work on them in there all the time. The house was on a dead-end street near the Assembly of God Church, where we went to at the time. I have so many wonderful memories there. The house was built on a hill, so I loved riding my bike up and down the hill, playing with my neighbor's grandchildren. My family coming over every Sunday after church and having dinner out of my dad's garden that my mom would cook. My dad had an awesome garden. It was behind our house in a field area to the left. He had a tractor he would plow it with. I enjoyed riding on it with him when I was young. It was my mom's dream home. I lived here until I got married.

I was so blessed to be born to such good parents. My dad was from a large family, there were eleven kids in his family, and he was the youngest son. He grew up working on his family farm. He never finished school because of the responsibilities on the farm.

He was so loving, and he always did extra things that made life special. He would get up early and fix my breakfast for me. If I was having cereal, he'd wait till I was coming down the hall and then pour the milk so my cereal would not get soggy. If it was cold outside, he'd have a fire in the fireplace and have my clothes lying in front of it so they would be warm. He always thought of the little things that made a big difference in your day. One thing I always enjoyed was coming into the kitchen and seeing my dad read his Bible. He taught me more about forgiveness than anyone.

My mom, she was great. She was the middle of five kids in her family. She had two older brothers and two younger sisters. I could always count on her to support me and be there. We had a unique bond; I think it's because it was just the two of us two for so many years together. She had such an incredible walk with the Lord. She would literally lay on the floor praying for hours a day. My mom said when she got saved, she didn't just get saved—she fell in love with Jesus. She taught me how to depend on Him through all of the things we went through and about my daily walk with the Lord. She also taught me how to love people. She was definitely the rock of our family. She had to be.

My brother, Thomas, and his wife had their son Eric when I was eighteen months old. I grew up with Eric, Tracey, and Tyra. We were all more like brother and sisters than my actual brothers and sisters. We did everything together. Most of my childhood photos are with them. My sister Lisa, who was ten years older than me, was my closest sibling growing up. When she got married, I cried for days. Not because I didn't like her husband, I was just so sad she was gone from home. She had a son, Christopher, when I was in high school, whom I spent a ton of time with. My brother, Kevin, was six years older. I adored him growing up. He was in middle school when I was in first and second grade. In our class, we'd go get milk from the lunchroom every day, and our teachers would pick different students to go get the milk. I would always be excited to go so I could see my brother during his lunch. He and his first wife had a son, Ryan, when I was in high school, three weeks before my sister's son was born. I literally did everything I could for those boys. I loved them so much, and they made my life wonderful.

The Fall

We moved into our home at Assembly Dr. when I was around nine months old. My dad was still finishing up some things on the new house. He was working on finishing the basement apartment out. The door going down to the basement had accidentally been left open. I was in my walker, and I somehow made my way to the steps. I fell down a full flight of steps going to our basement. The stairs did not have walls or railing on either side, yet I went straight down and hit a concrete block wall at the bottom instead of falling off. I had a huge knot on my head. It was a miracle I didn't fall off the side of the steps! My mom would tell me the story of how she was heading to the hospital, but my dad was like, "No, Dot, this is something for God to handle. We are going to pray." So pray they did all night and kept me awake. God brought me through it, and I never had any issues. The Lord had His hand on me!

Then, when I was in middle school, I went to get an eye exam. The doctor doing the exam saw a scar on my eye and wanted to know what it was from. He said it was probably from a fall of some sort. My mom and I couldn't figure it out, so as we were talking to him, she realized it was from that fall. He was amazed. He said that if it had literally been a hair over, like a piece of hair, I would have been blind in that eye! Imagine a piece of hair, and I would never have seen out of that eye most of my life. That would have changed my life drastically. Even to this day, when he does my eye exams, he shakes his head in amazement. If you don't think God has it under control and has His hand on you, He does. Look, that day could have turned out totally different in so many ways, yet He protected me even down to my vision. And if it had turned out differently, God would have still been there to help me through it. Things don't always go as we want them to, but God is always there, even when we don't feel Him or see Him. We have to trust Him.

Oh My God, No!

When I was born, my dad owned a heating and air conditioning company called Sanford Heating and Air. He was one of the first people to start putting A/C units in people's homes in the late sixties. He was extremely good at his job, and his customers loved him. He would get up at any time of night and go fix someone's heat or air. He couldn't stand to think they were too hot or too cold. Unfortunately, he ended up with a hernia and had to close the business. He could no longer lift the heavy units.

My dad, being the entrepreneur he was, opened a small grocery store in Monkey Town, an area in Cartersville just about ten minutes from our home. Back in the '70s, they had little stores with small amounts of groceries, and my dad opened one and had the best meat in town!

I remember being a child and going into the store and getting candy. The candy was near the front of the store, to the right on a shelf. The meat was in the back part of the store, and the register area was in the front, near where you walked into the building. I remember very little about it since I was so young. It was a brick building with windows at the top along the side.

On a very cold Georgia Saturday night, January 17, 1976, my brother, Kevin, who was ten years old at the time, was standing at the register while my dad was walking around the store to close up. My dad would walk around every night and make sure everything was turned off and locked up. As my dad got back to the front of the store, this black man was standing at the door with a Molotov cocktail bomb in his hand. Typically, my dad walked around the store with his gun, but that night he did not. I'm not really sure why, but I like to think it's because as bad as everything was, the good Lord knew my dad couldn't handle it if he had killed someone.

My dad told my brother to throw him the gun, and when he did, the guy threw the bomb at my dad, it hit him on the hip area, and it exploded. My dad was on fire, the store was on fire, and my brother's leg was on fire! Everything was burning!

There was a cooler in the back of the store that had just started to leak water that my dad had not had time to fix that weekend. My brother heard my dad tell him to go roll in the water from the cooler. Of course, my dad didn't say it; he wasn't able to do anything but scream from being on fire himself. It was God! I can't imagine what it was like for my brother, especially being so young, to know the building was on fire, to hear my dad screaming because he was burning, the reality and fear of all of that to a kid. But I do know that God was there because He spoke to my brother to roll in the water. He had other plans for his life. My family felt the consequences of the fire forever, especially my dad and brother. Growing up, I didn't realize the impact it had on my brother until I got older, but I know God had to have His hand on him for him to come through it.

Some people were driving by the store that night and saw it was on fire and stopped to help and called the fire department. They broke out the windows and tried to control the fire with water hoses. Unfortunately, it just made it worst by feeding it more oxygen. It didn't matter, though; they were still heroes trying to help my dad and my brother.

I'll never forget that night. I was four years old. My mom and I had been snapping green beans and been watching our Saturday night lineup of The Love Boat, Fantasy Island ("The plane, the plane!"), and then the news. The Love Boat was one of my favorite TV shows, and I still enjoy it to this day. The news had just gone off when the phone rang. She walked into the kitchen area from our den to answer the phone, and all I heard was, "Oh my God, *no*!" After that, everything was a blur; I only remember the E.R. and the many, many days of being at the hospital.

My dad had 65 percent of his body burned with third-degree burns. My brother's leg was burned right above his ankle, several inches all the way around his leg. His leg was in traction in his hospital bed, and my dad was bandaged from head to toe. My mom had to sneak me in to see my dad because I was so young. Every time a nurse came in, I'd run into the bathroom and hide. Seeing my dad and brother like that is something I have never forgotten.

The doctor on duty the night of the fire had no burn experience and was not doing such a great job with my dad and brother. He would come in and rip off the crusted flesh. My mom found out about a doctor that had not been in Cartersville long but was from the JMS Burn Center in Augusta, Georgia. She had to fight legally to have the first doctor removed so this doctor could take over my dad and brother as patients. Thank the Lord he had sent this doctor to our little town right before my dad's burn. Again, it shows you how even when you don't realize it, God is in the midst of it, preparing the way for you. God was showing up before we even knew we needed Him to.

My dad had several operations and skin grafts. He lost two fingers on his left hand and one on his right hand. He was in the hospital for months. It took a long time to recover from such an awful burn. God used Dr. Davis to save my dad's life. If he hadn't been in Cartersville when this happened, my dad would not have been around to see me grow up. My dad was, of course, disabled from then on out. He had to teach himself to pick stuff up again because he couldn't feel anything. I remember watching him as he had to literally watch his hand to make sure it was touching the item, to make sure he was picking it up. He would do certain things and not even realize he had cut himself or hit his arm and it was bleeding. I would ask why he was bleeding, and he'd have no idea he was. It was hard! He was so used to going and doing and working and then not being able to. He was able to drive once he recovered. My dad could work on anything before he was burned. He was great with cars. My brother ended up being one of the best car mechanics because my dad taught him how to do what he could not do anymore.

This was the beginning of my knowing who God was and the process of watching my dad learn to forgive the man who burned him and my brother.

We almost lost everything. I remember going through town and seeing people from different churches in town standing at the traffic lights collecting money for my family. In the '70s, that was a typical way to help someone in your community that really needed help. And we really needed help. My dad's store insurance had just lapsed, and my mom wasn't able to work because my dad was so bad. By God's grace, we survived!

The guy who burnt my dad turned himself in a few weeks after he did it. He said he would sit on the train tracks at the overpass right next to my dad's store and watch him and planned it for months. He went to trial. I remember going to the trial for one day. It was in our county courthouse. I remember a judge sitting on the bench and people sitting on the side of the courtroom in chairs. I was sitting with my mom. The room was mainly a light wood. I don't remember anything about the trial, though; I was so young. Unfortunately, they deemed him mentally ill and sent him to a mental hospital in Milledgeville, Georgia, two times. Both times, they sent him back, saying nothing was wrong, so he walked. I'm sure his uncle being a lawyer helped.

My dad and brother really suffered for a long time, and my family as well. Everything we knew before was gone. I remember one day riding down Old Mill Road in Cartersville, this was near my school, in my dad's little S-10 truck, and my dad telling me how he had forgiven the guy that burned him and my brother. He said it was hard to do, but he knew it was the Christian thing to do. It took him a long time to get to that point.

Saying Goodbye Is Hard

We used to travel almost every summer to Albuquerque, New Mexico. My Aunt Dru and Uncle Grady lived there (my mom's oldest brother and his wife). They were my favorite aunt and uncle. I loved going to Albuquerque. One of my favorite things was the drive out, stopping at hotels on the way and stopping early enough for me to swim. We stayed at mom-and-pop hotels then; it was the mid-late '70s and early '80s. We would typically travel through Alabama, Mississippi, and Louisiana. A few times, we stopped in Beaumont, Texas, to see Bo. She was an older lady who had lived in our basement apartment for a while, Bo wasn't her real name, but it was what I called her. I always loved her because she was like a grandmother figure to me. She ended up moving back to Texas, so my parents went a few times to see her on our way to Dallas. It was definitely out of the way! I loved traveling on the interstate and driving into big cities. It always left me in awe. My dad would always make sure I was awake when we were about to come into a big city so I could see it. It also took longer to drive because the speed limit was fifty-five. Can you imagine? Fifty-five!

The trip I remember the most was this trip, though. It was July 1982. We were in our custom van. We stopped in Mississippi at a hotel the first night. We went next door to a local restaurant to eat; then, I went swimming. My dad would sit out by the pool and watch me while I swam. We always stopped in Dallas, Texas, at my cousin Rick and Vivan's house. That night we got in late to their house. It was 103°F, so you guessed it, I went swimming in their pool. I loved stopping at their house. They also had four boys around my age, so I always enjoyed seeing them.

A funny story. Since Rick had the four boys, he was always conscious of the thermostat. My dad got hot and was having trouble breathing since he had been burned, and it had affected his lungs so badly. He would get up after everyone was in bed and would hold his lighter under the thermostat to make the air come on. In a little bit, Rick would come and check it to see if it had been changed, and it wasn't. My dad would chuckle.

We would then head to New Mexico. I loved the drive into Albuquerque, through the mountain, and then seeing the city. The city was huge, and seeing the lights at night coming over the mountain was beautiful. I still love it to this day. My aunt and uncle had a cute three-bedroom, two-bath home across from the fairground and within walking distance from a McDonald's. As a kid, I always loved that! They had two little dogs, and she always had soda in the garage. Aunt Dru would make homemade tortillas with butter for breakfast. Oh, how I wish I had learned to make them! I loved Albuquerque; it was like a second home to me. We had talked about moving there since it was easier for him to breathe in the dry heat than the humid Georgia heat, but he would never leave his kids; they were his world.

As far back as I can remember, my aunt Dru always took us to Old Town, which I still love to this day and have taken my daughter to several times. Old Town has stores around a square and a neat catholic church on one corner with a park-like setting in the middle. My mom would always buy a piece of turquoise jewelry from there, the Native Americans would set up on the sidewalk on the ground and lay out their jewelry on blankets (they still do). We would eat at La Hacienda. I always thought it was so cool because it had a tree growing in the middle of the restaurant, and the food was so good.

The Sandia Mountains were beautiful, especially at sunset when they turned pink. *Sandia* means "watermelon" in Spanish. My aunt Dru would also take us to an Indian reservation to get the best bread around. I loved going and seeing how they lived and the ovens they cooked bread in. The reservations were dirt roads with little houses next to each other. Most of them had their stoves outside of the house. The reservation I remember the most was on a small mountain.

I think Mexican food is my favorite food to this day because of having it there. Even though it tastes different there, I loved it; I wish we had some like it in the south. My other favorite thing is the *sopapillas* they have. Every time we'd go to eat and get sopapillas, Aunt Dru would call them "sofa pillows" because they looked like a small pillow. I always laughed at her joke, even though she's right, they look like tiny sofa pillows! They are about the size of your hand. They bring them out warm, and you open them up and pour honey into them. Oh my goodness, one of the best things ever! Every time we visit, even now, I have to go get "sofa pillows"! Nowhere else have I ever found them like they do them in New Mexico.

We would stay with Aunt Dru and Uncle Grady for a week or two and then travel somewhere else, like Nevada, Colorado, or Wyoming. This is why I have such a love for the West. I have some of my best memories from growing up while traveling with my family. Back then, we didn't always travel highways, so there was so much more to see on the smaller roads. I loved seeing dust storms, they used to scare me at first because they looked like a tornado and tumble weeds blowing in the desert.

My dad had a CB; his name was "Road Runner." He was always on it talking to truckers, finding out where cops were, how the traffic was, etc. I loved talking with truckers also. We always had a good time. He'd drink his Pepsi, eat his pork skins, drive the van (it was the nice custom van, with captain seats that turned and a small table, plus a couch-like seat that made into a bed in the back), and talk on the CB. It was so much fun. I loved the movie "Smokie and the Bandit," I think it's because it reminded me so much of our trips out west. My dad and I would watch it together.

In late July 1982, we went to Albuquerque and stayed with Aunt Dru and Uncle Grady. We then all went to Las Vegas for a few nights. The first night we went to Circus Circus, my aunt had my face painted. I was so tired that night, though, that by the time we got back to our room, I was crying and messing up my face paint. We then went on to Reno for a week. We were in Reno for a convention for my mom's job. We went to Lake Tahoe, where they filmed the TV show Bonanza. It was so cool to see where they would come down the hill. On the show, it looked like a huge hill; instead, it was very small and short. When we were leaving, Uncle Grady put a coin in the slot machine and won! Money was going everywhere (that's when they weren't digital). We were grabbing money and putting it in our shirts, pockets, etc., and so was everyone else.

My dad loved that trip. When we got back from that trip, I found out my fantail goldfish had died. My goldfish was huge;

he was around seven or eight inches long and beautiful. He was three years old, and I loved it. The house had gotten a little too hot that summer, and he didn't make it. A week later, I started 7th grade.

My dad would always take me to school. His dog Shane, which was a white poodle, would ride with us. Shane loved my dad; he stayed by his side all day and slept beside him in his bed every night. He was so funny; he would get in the bed with my dad and lay his head on the other pillow, my dad would cover him up to his neck with the covers, and he would sleep there. He would also growl at you when you tried to give my dad a hug! He was his protector, or so he thought. My dad typically took me to school because he was the early riser, and my mom loved to sleep in. It was the first day of my 7th-grade year, and we were running late. We were so late that there were barely any other cars dropping off. I got to school, and I jumped out of the truck, running. As I got to the front door, I realized I had not told my dad I loved him, but he was already pulling off in his little black S-10 truck. I always told my mom and dad I loved them when leaving them, I think because of what I had already been through. When I got out of school that day, I found out that when he dropped me off, he went to get milk at the Golden Gallon, not far from our house, and on his way, he went into congestive heart failure. He ended up wrecking his truck into this older lady's house. Poor thing, it really shook her up. Shane got out during all of it but was found and returned to us, thank goodness. My dad was in ICU and on a ventilator. Seeing him lying there with tubes everywhere, unresponsive, was devastating.

I knew he was bad, but I was twelve, and I had no idea how bad it really was or that I was about to lose him forever.

I was in ICU with my dad one day, and there was a storm. The power went out, and as the generator kicked in, his machine made some noise. I remember I screamed because it scared me, and I took off running. The nurses told my mom they were thankful I screamed, or they would not have realized so quickly that something had happened to his machine through the outage. It scared me so bad I thought something was happening to him with me right there. He eventually got out of ICU but was put in a room right next to the nurse's station. His eyes were open, but he couldn't talk. He would just look at you and follow you around the room. I remember his sweet eyes watching me as I talked to him. You could tell he knew you and what you were saying. His lips would get so dry that my mom would swab them. He wasn't in this room but a few days. My mom was with him when he passed. She had told him it was okay, she didn't want to see him suffer anymore, and that we would be okay. She said it wasn't long after that.

On September 12, 1982, I was at school in my science class. I remember getting this sickening feeling and looking at the clock on the wall. I knew he was gone. I could just feel it. A few hours later, my mom came and picked me up. When I saw her, I knew my feelings were confirmed. I asked her when he had passed, and she told me the time. It was the same time that I looked at the clock. She was trying to be strong, but she was crying. My mom didn't cry much. That was one of the longest walks to our car I ever had. My world was rocked. I lost my dad, my dad, who I was so close to, especially since he was home from being disabled. I was blessed and got to spend more time with him than most twelve-year-olds. I was heartbroken and couldn't believe I would never see him again. How do you go on at twelve without your dad? Let me tell you, it was hard! It was just my mom and me. It was at this point that I learned to trust the Lord as not only my savior but my Father.

Cartersville was a small town, and my dad knew just about everyone. He was loved by so many. So much is a blur to me, but I remember the funeral home was packed. It was at Owen's Funeral Home on Main Street in Cartersville, which is now the police station. We had his funeral at Cartersville Church of God on Old Mill Road, and our pastor preached it. The church sat over 1,200, and it was packed with people standing in the back. My dad was only fifty-four; he would have been fifty-five on September 19th. He died on my sister's second wedding anniversary and a week before his birthday. The day we buried my dad, his dog Shane was let out to go potty and got attacked by another dog and also died. I knew my dad just wanted Shane with him. They were best buds, and I don't think Shane would have survived without my dad. He was already having a hard time with him not being at home.

The days, weeks, and months after he passed were so hard. I actually failed Home Ec, and my grades suffered horribly. I missed my dad so much. If life wasn't bad enough, I was bullied at school by a girl that would make fun of me every day. As I walked down the hall, she'd say the building was shaking. Funny thing is that I wasn't really overweight, but I was tall. I was going through hell every day without the added junk. Middle school was definitely rough for me. I hated it! My saving grace was my youth group. I went to my first function not too long after my dad passed. I ended up having a great time and making so many new friends. It helped me through so much.

My emotions were so high my mom and I would argue. It was an adjustment not having my dad around. I remember one day, I was so mad at everything that I threw my brush across the room and slammed the door. I was angry, I was hurting, I missed my dad! I never thought about what my mom was going through, I just knew I was hurting, even though during my dad's funeral, I had one of his cousins tell me I shouldn't cry, I needed to be strong for my mom. Who tells a twelve-year-old that? My mom definitely didn't feel that way. She did the best she could and was very supportive of me. I truly don't know how she did it except with the Lord's help.

I'd be in our den watching the Brady Bunch; I'd hear my dad come in the door and turn and then realize it was no one. Or I'd be cutting grass, and I'd hear his truck drive up and be excited to see him, then realize he wasn't there. It was weird; I'd get excited to tell him something or see him, and then it would hit me that it was not going to happen. He was usually sitting at the kitchen table or on the back screened-in porch reading his Bible every morning. I missed seeing him there doing that.

I missed him at all of my big and small things, like my sixteenth birthday, seeing me in my prom dress, graduating high school, walking me down the aisle at my wedding, meeting my husband, Terry, whom he would have loved, and, most importantly, being there when my daughter Carmen was born, not getting to hold her and meet her as she grew up. He would have enjoyed her so much. I hate that she missed him too; that's been a big loss for her.

I knew he wasn't suffering, but to a twelve-year-old, that really didn't make too much sense. I wondered why God didn't heal him here on earth. At these times, you realize there's always a reason, even if we don't ever understand. He was only fifty-four. But I did know where he was, which made me want to have a stronger relationship with the Lord. I wanted to make sure I saw him again one day.

Dealing with Fear

I think because of everything I had been through so far, I was very fearful. I used to be afraid to go into my house; I was always scared someone was in the house hiding somewhere. I'd sit in the car in our car porch, and my poor mom had to go in before me and check every door, under every bed, and in every closet every time we came in. Every night we would put a chair under our kitchen door to make sure no one could get in, and she or I would go around to every door and make sure they were all locked. In the kitchen, with the blinds we had, you couldn't see onto our screened-in back porch, and I never wanted to, so I'd stick my hand behind the blind and check the door and then walk away in case someone was there. I was afraid someone would be looking in at me. It was a real fear that was horrible to deal with. I also didn't like staying by myself because of it. Then, one day, God showed me Psalm 27:1: "The Lord is my light and my salvation, Whom shall I fear? The Lord is the strength of my life; Of whom shall I be afraid?" This verse, when I read it, grabbed ahold of my life, and I started quoting it every day, every time fear would come in.

I would go into my house and quote my verse on fear, trusting the Lord to help me and protect me. I memorized the verse so I could use it as a weapon against the enemy as he tried to paralyze me with fear. I remember staying by myself for the first time one night while my mom had plans. Of course, I heard every sound you could hear, but to know that I was able to overcome this with the Lord's help was such a relief; I was getting my life back. It was like a breath of fresh air. This is the reason we should read our Bible, learn verses, and hide them in our hearts, so when we go to battle with the enemy, especially in our minds, we have weapons from the Holy Spirit to fight the devil with. Another form of fear I had to fight, which was a little harder, was always worrying about losing my mom. This was a different fear, so I had to trust the Lord daily with this. When I was fourteen, my mom had a spot come up on her leg that ended up being a bone infection. I was scared; I had just lost my dad almost two years before. I was worried I was going to lose her too. It was a very serious infection. It was a little weird because on her left ankle as a small kid, she had had a bone infection, and typically it should have been on that leg; instead, it was up on her right thigh. She had surgery in late spring that did not do what it needed to. That surgery was rough on her and me. They left the area going to her bone open; it was a hole that was about two inches long and one inch wide. We had to clean it several times a day. I had to remove the gauze and throw them away, then put something like Betadine in the wound, then repack it. It would stink so badly. I didn't mind doing it, but could you imagine that being your responsibility at fourteen years old? I know she was suffering from the pain. I loved my mom and would do anything for her. She had a convention in Washington, DC, that we went to even with her leg like it was. She was so strong. I can't imagine doing that. I'd get up every morning and do her leg and every night before bed.

Dealing with Fear

She only went to the convention because she wasn't able to do anything else. Sometimes she'd grab something to eat with her friends. Times were so different back then. I'd go by myself to places near the hotel where we stayed. I don't know if I'd let my nineteen-year-old do that today! We stayed at the J. W. Marriott. It has a map in the park across the street from it that I loved to go to every day. I'd either swim with friends I made while she was at the convention, or I'd go to what they called the mall; it's a place with a lot of different walk-up restaurants.

My sister Lisa found this doctor at St. Joseph's Hospital in Atlanta that specialized in bone infections and had created a new procedure that was perfect for my mom. When we met him, my mom and I couldn't get over how much he favored her nephew, Rick. The procedure was antibiotics in these things that looked like pearls. He would go in, scrape the infection from her bone, and then leave these pearl-like things in to dissolve with the antibiotic in them. It worked very well. I was so grateful for him and how the Lord used him to help my mom. If God had not led us to this doctor, things could have been different again, yet God worked it out for her. I shared this story, even though I didn't go into as much detail, because it was something very hard in my life to see my mom go through and the fear that I lived through during this time. It was things like this that made my mom and I so close.

My House Is on Fire

On Saturday, January 18, 1986, my mom cooked us some steaks on our grill on our back screened-in porch. I had called a friend of mine, Shelby, to come to spend the night, and last minute she was able to, so we ran over the hill literally to pick her up. A few hours later, I decided to take a shower because of church the next morning. While I was in the shower, I heard someone banging on our front door. I was worried and scared as I turned off the shower to see what was going on. All I could hear was my mom screaming, "Oh God, my house is on *fire*!"

Our neighbors from behind our house (remember, we were on almost two acres of land) daughter was there late, handling some family stuff because they had just lost her grandfather. She happened to look up and saw that our big screened-in back porch was on fire, blazing. She told her family to call the fire department as she took off running to our house. At this point, the fire was still outside. She started banging on our front door. No one ever came to our front door, so when I heard the banging, I thought someone was breaking into our house. As my mom opened the front door, Brenda was trying to pull her out, and my mom was trying to get her into the house, thinking she was in danger. Then, she finally got my mom to realize our house was on fire! At that point, my mom walked to our kitchen to go "see" how bad the fire was. We had those roll-down blinds on the doors that were popular in the '80s, so she really couldn't see the fire, but as she was about to open the sliding glass door and she literally had her hand on the latch unlocking it, my dad's voice came back to her saying that during his fire at the store, if they hadn't broken the windows, the fire would not have spread so fast, so she removed her hand and walked away. The firefighter told her that if she had opened it, it would have engulfed her and killed her. Again, God showed up and saved my mom's life, even in the midst of the fire!

I got out of the shower with shampoo in my hair, pulling my nightgown on as I headed out the front door with my mom and Shelby. My mom had a renter in the basement at the time, and we couldn't get to her from the basement door. So, my mom went back into the house and down the stairs to get her; about that time, the renter came out of the basement door, so I ran back into the burning house to get my mom. I remember the smoke along the ceiling as I paused to look at the den and hearing the glass door by my dad's chair break from the fire as my mom and I were running back out. We had black soot from the smoke on us, and we had inhaled a good bit of smoke, so we had to go to the hospital later on. We stood out on the street with our pastor watching our home burn as the firefighters put it out. I was so thankful to see my dog Rosie was okay. She was deaf. Rosie had been Kevin's dog, but my dad loved her, so having her was like having something of my dad's. It was absolutely heartbreaking watching my home burn! All of the fire trucks and lights from the emergency vehicles, along with the fire and smoke from the house, lit up the night sky. I remember standing there, crying as it burned. All my memories, especially of my dad, were vanishing before my eyes. Another loss, yet again, another opportunity for me to realize who God is and the peace He gives you in the middle of the storm.

That night when we left to pick up Shelby, my mom had been cooking us a steak on the grill. It was a natural gas grill, she turned it off, but in her rush, she forgot to turn the gas off. In a natural gas grill, the gas is from the gas line, not from a propane tank, so after a while, it caught the back porch on fire because it was so hot.

The fire was called a surface fire, which means it burns everything on the surface and keeps going. It burned our kitchen really badly, part of our laundry room, some of our living/dining room, and our den; everything was burned: our foyer and down our hall. What wasn't ruined with fire was ruined with water and smoke damage.

One thing I'll never forget was my dad's Bible. The next day, when we went back into the house to see the damage, in the kitchen, literally in the most intense part of the fire near the sliding doors where the fire came in, was my dad's Bible. The leather was burned, and the edges of the pages were charred, but not a word was burned! Can you imagine? Not a word! If you don't believe, there's power in the Word of God!

We pretty much lost everything. The only thing that we really had left was my mom and dad's bedroom suit and her dining room set. She was able to have them cleaned, and I still have her bedroom set to this day!

Again, I was devasted! Everything I got for Christmas was gone. All my clothes, toys, Barbie dolls I was saving for my child one day, my memories, etc... We had kept my dad's clothes, but they were gone. But one thing that wasn't gone was some of our pictures that were in a table by my dad's chair. Because it was a surface fire, they were saved! They had some smoke and water damage, but they were okay. The outside wood on the table was ruined with the fire, but the content was okay in the drawer. It's things like this where you see God's hand over and over in the midst of the storm. See, life happens; it rains on the just and the unjust (Matthew 5:45). It's just we, followers of Christ, have His peace to get us through it all. That doesn't mean we don't feel the effects because we do, believe me, but it does mean we have peace deep down in our spirit.

It's funny how certain things stand out. I remember walking into my home the morning after the fire, and it was destroyed. I just stood there and cried, looking at my home, my memories. It was awful! My heart hurt so bad. We had to write down everything for insurance purposes. So many special things were lost, even things that were little, like a sweater I got in Gatlinburg. I loved this sweater; it was sleeveless, aqua-blue, and knitted. My mom and I, and usually some of her friends, would always go up Christmas day and stay for a few nights to make the Christmas season last longer. It defiantly changes the way you feel about material things when you lose them all. For me, I learned they were things and life is more important; I'm sure for someone else, it may make them want to cling to them more.

Then the builders came in and started tearing everything out on the inside. When I walked into what was once my home since I was a baby, it was now gutted. My memories with my dad, the stuff he had built, would never be again. My home was just a shell. As the house started being rebuilt, I started having fun picking out new wallpaper and carpet. My mom took some room out of the guest bedroom closet and made me a desk with "Hollywood lights," that's what I called them. This was really special to me. I loved it because she had it done for me. She bought me a bed that was an antique bed; it was a high-back bed that was over one hundred years old. I loved it and still have it. I also played piano, so she got me a telephone for my room that was the shape of a baby grand piano. And she got me another piano which I have to this day, to actually play.

It took eleven months to rebuild our house because the builder and the insurance adjuster were in cahoots together and ran off with our insurance money. We had to sue them to get $10 a week, which was a joke, and to get them to release the furniture they had in storage back to us. Thank goodness my mom had the little bit of money that we had gotten from the insurance company to buy clothes and furniture with to finish out the house.

My sister, Lisa, and her husband let us live with them for the entire eleven months. I was so thankful; I can only imagine what it was like to have your in-laws move in with you, especially under such hard circumstances, and a fourteen-year-old, almost fifteen-year-old at that. This kept us from having to live in a hotel or rent an apartment. It was comforting having them around (plus my sister is a great cook), especially when we had already lost everything.

My home burned ten years pretty much to the date that my dad's store had burned. His store was a Saturday night on January 17, 1976, and my house was a Saturday night on January 18, 1986.

The Wreck

It was fall after my house had burned, and I was back in school. I was fifteen years old and in tenth grade. I was never a big fan of school, not even as a kid. As a matter of fact, I hated school so bad I'd throw up every morning until I reached fourth grade. It was a mixture of my sinuses and my fear of leaving my parents. I cried every morning going to kindergarten and first grade just because I wanted to be with my mom and dad. I think my dad being burned and going through that trauma made me want to be with them.

It was a Friday in September; we were having a pep rally that day for our football game that night. I did enjoy the pep rallies; they were fun. I remember sitting in the pep rally and knowing something was wrong, but I had no idea what it was, so I just prayed! I prayed for protection over me, my mom, my family, and anything else I could think of. I was so unrestful. So, I just plead the blood of Jesus and His protection over us; that's all I knew to do. I did this the entire time I was in the pep rally.

When school was out, I went out front for my mom to pick me up, and instead, my sister, Lisa, and my mom's younger sister, Aunt Frankie, were with my mom. My aunt had just gotten a brand new 1986 Monte Carlo. It was like a-few-days-old brand new. It was pretty, and she was so proud of it.

I got in the back seat behind my aunt. She was taking us home—well, to my sister's because we were still living with her. I didn't get to see her a lot, so I was super excited to see her. We were driving up Highway 41 in Cartersville. It's a four-lane highway with red lights. We were at the intersection of 41 and Felton Road, and all of a sudden, a truck ran the red light and t-boned us on my side of the car, right in the driver's door. Everything was in slow motion; Frankie's head hit the driver's door window really hard. As soon as we stopped moving, I could see smoke, and I heard this noise that sounded like a fire. I went into complete panic mode; my adrenaline kicked in, and the next thing I knew I had kicked my aunt's door open and gotten out of the car. As soon as I was out, I realized the car wasn't on fire, but all of the fluids were leaking from the car, making the noise that sounded like it was. I have to admit, I was relieved. As we were standing there, the fire department showed up with the cops and an ambulance, and I remember the fireman asking how we got the driver's door open. He couldn't figure out how it was opened; he said it should have never opened with the way it was hit. I guess between my adrenaline and the good Lord helping me, it came open.

Aunt Frankie's car was totaled. Remember, it was brand new, and it was totaled! We all walked out of that wreck okay, with no serious injuries. It was a miracle, but unfortunately, it was more trauma after just eight months of having lost my home in the fire.

I know if I had not obeyed the Holy Spirit that day and prayed the entire time during the pep rally, I believe it would have been a lot worse. Again, God's protection was on our lives.

The Girls

I graduated from Cartersville High School on June 4, 1989. I couldn't wait to be out of school. As I said before, I hated school. My saving grace was my church youth group. Our youth pastor and his wife were the best. Tony and Barbara Jacobs. I loved them, our youth group, and our youth workers. Especially the Goss's, Ron and June, who opened their home to us all the time. We had afterglows and Bible study after church on Sunday nights. Afterglows were just get-togethers at a leader's house with snacks to hang out with other youths. It was such a great way to bond, have great memories, and stay out of trouble (most of the time).

A month after I graduated, I started cosmetology school in Marietta. I had always wanted to do hair, even when I was six years old. I'd cut and play with my dolls' hair. I had such a great opportunity come up. Karen was in our singles group at church, and she cut hair in Vinings, Georgia, at Bob Steele Hairdressers. It was a top-notch salon. I was able to start assisting her on Saturdays and Thursday nights to make sure this was really what I wanted to do, and it was! In my last quarter at school, we were allowed to work in a salon several days a week, so I worked under Karen. She was amazing and taught me everything I knew about hair and clients.

My sister Linda had two daughters. Tracey was born on March 14, 1969, right at a week of being two years before I was born. Her sister Tyra was born on February 20, 1971, three weeks before me.

We grew up together, we celebrated our birthdays together, played together, and fought together. We were like sisters, more than their mother and I were. My sister was eighteen years older than me, so we really weren't that close.

They moved to Marietta when they were in elementary school because of my sister's job. She had been married when she had them but had gotten a divorce when she was twenty-one. So, she was a single mom raising her two girls. My mom and dad had helped her a ton when they were younger. She lived in the house on Pine Street (the house I was brought home to as a baby) with the girls. Marietta was about forty-five minutes from my home, so we would see them but not every day like I was used to. I'd go spend the night with them sometimes, and they'd come to my house too. As they got older, my sister moved to Kennesaw, which was closer to us, so they were like twenty minutes away instead of forty-five minutes.

In high school, the girls got involved with some rougher guys and truthfully gave my sister a hard time. She did everything she could, and the thing she did best was love them no matter what. We, of course, grew apart with them being further away and dating the guys they were. But I still loved them and kept in touch.

Eventually, Tracey and Tyra moved out of my sister's house and got an apartment in Marietta. They both ended up pregnant but were trying to get their lives together. Their apartment was only a few miles from my job, so once the babies were born, I'd

The Girls

go by see them and help them cut their nails. Tracey had a boy, he was born on July 27, 1989, and Tyra had Destiny, who was born in October. I don't remember her birthday. They were both so cute! Tyra worked, and Tracey would stay at home with the babies; they were great moms, doing the best they could.

It was MLK day, Monday, January 15th, 1990. We were out of school, and I didn't work on Mondays. I was supposed to meet the girls at my sister's house in Kennesaw to give Tyra a perm and cut Tracey's hair. I was excited because I was going to get to see the babies! I had not heard from them yet that morning. My mom was a real estate agent so she had ran to work and I was watching my two nephews, which I loved.

I had had a rough weekend. On Saturday, I kept having unrest and started praying—and I mean praying! I was literally on my face, banging my fist, pleading, and praying because I felt death. Truthfully, I thought it was my mom I was going to lose. I was so scared; I have had feelings to pray for things all of my life, but this was different. I knew it was death; I kept praying and praying and rebuking the enemy. That Sunday night, I dreamed that Tracey was pregnant again, and I was so upset with her.

While I was watching my nephews (they were two years old), I was talking with a friend on the phone. That's when we had home phones with call waiting. I had a call come in, so I clicked over, and it was my niece's aunt from their dad's side. She was asking me if we had heard anything about the girls. Which we had not because they had not located my sister yet, so she proceeded to tell me they had been killed. I had no idea how, what, when... I was a mess! I was thinking they were in a car wreck. I was trying to reach my family, and truthfully, I don't remember much else except getting to my sister's house and waiting for her friend from work to bring her home. It was *awful*! When she got there, I remember her falling into my mom's arms, wailing. It was horrific. We were all a mess. There's nothing like the cry of a mom over her children being taken too soon. She not only lost a child but both children, Tracey and Tyra, and Destiny, the three-month-old baby. Tracey was twenty, and Tyra was eighteen. We all stayed with her all night, along with our pastor, even though he wasn't at our church anymore. When the news came on showing the story and carrying their bodies out on the gurney, I felt like I was in a nightmare, and I just wanted to wake up, but I couldn't—it was real. It was a real-life nightmare. The girls who I grew up with, whom we shared most of our childhood birthdays and Christmases together, and I was getting a second chance at rebuilding our relationship with, were gone forever.

It was MLK day, and Tyra's ex-boyfriend, Destiny's dad, was off work, as was Tyra. He was already living with another girl. He got up that morning and wrote a letter to his girlfriend telling her what he was going to do. He left, went to a pawn shop, bought a gun, and headed to the girl's apartment. He went to the door and knocked, and they were there with the babies, some friends, and Tracey's boyfriend. Just as he got to the apartment, his girlfriend called and asked for him. He told her he was okay, that he was just upset that morning when he wrote the note, and hung up the phone. Tyra was in her bedroom, so he went back to see her; the baby was in her crib. They started arguing, so Tracey went in to get the baby. Remember she didn't know about the note and the girlfriend didn't say anything to anyone, just to him. As she got in there, all we could figure out was that he either had the gun out or pulled it out, but the next thing they knew was they heard a gunshot. Tracy's boyfriend took off down the hall to see what was going on, and he shot at him, so he ducked into their son's room and locked the door, and called 911. He ended up shooting Tyra two times, Tracey once in the head, and the baby two times in the stomach. How can someone do this? I mean, as Christians, we know how—they are lost, but still. How do you shoot your own baby two times? Thankfully for us, he went to his car and reloaded his gun and shot himself in the head. I prayed he was able to repent for what he had done, but I was thankful we didn't have to go to court over this; it was so hard already.

They had to do autopsies since they were so young, and we had to wait until that Wednesday to have visitation. That was on January 17, 1990, fifteen years from the day my dad's store burned. We had it at Jennings Funeral Home in Cartersville. We already knew so many people, but due to the circumstances, everyone wanted to let us know they supported us. We had so many people, they had to send cops out to direct traffic all evening. I'll never forget Tyra holding sweet Destiny in her arms; they were so peaceful lying there.

That Thursday, January 18th, was their funeral. I'll never forget getting in the limo, going to the church, following both hearses, crying, and hurting. Then, I remember riding down Cassville Road, and all of a sudden, peace hit me. It was then that I knew exactly what the verse in Philippians 4:6 meant: "Instead, in every situation with prayer and petition, with thanksgiving, tell your request to God. And the peace that surpasses all understanding will guard your hearts and minds in Christ Jesus." My hurt and pain were still there; my grief was still there, but I had peace in midst of the storm.

The church was packed, just like when my dad's funeral was there. That was a really hard walk down that aisle. As kids, we would sing "Amazing Grace," so that was sung at the funeral. Pastor May did the funeral, but I don't remember anything else. Not even the graveside.

I remember going back to work that Saturday, and I'm not really sure how I did it. I don't think I could have really been of any help, but somehow, I made it. I remember days driving down the road and thinking if I wrecked and died, my pain would be gone. But through God's love, peace, and mercy, He brought me through it.

That same year my oldest brother, Thomas, was diagnosed with prostate cancer. When the doctor went in to do surgery, he had said he thought he would be eaten up with it; instead, there wasn't that much, and he was able to do only radiation. My brother Kevin and his wife got a divorce that year too. Nineteen-ninety was a rough year for us. But God! God got us through it.

As I look back over just these few things, I know the only way I have made it through was with Jesus Christ and His grace. Remember, it rains on the just and the unjust the same. It's just whether you have God's peace to get you through it all or not. His peace is real; His presence is real. If you don't know Him, please turn your heart to Him today; let Him give you peace. Let Him show you who He is. He loves you and wants to be a part of your life.

My Family

On New Year's Eve 1992, I had plans with a friend of mine that was in town for the holidays from the military. Last minute, he got called back to base, so my plans changed, and I ended up going to a singles group NYE service at Lawrenceville Church of God with my single group instead. It was there that I met my husband, Terry. Terry was the lead singer in a band that was playing at the service at his church. After the service that night, we got to talking. He called me the next day, and the rest is history. We had been dating for two years and ten months before we got married. We got married on October 7, 1995, and were blessed with an awesome wedding, even though it was a little stressful the few days before. We lived in North Georgia, but a hurricane had hit Panama City, Florida, and kept on coming, so once it reached our city, there were still 100 mph winds. Our caterer was without power, the lady making our cakes was without power, and the house we were having a reception at had trees down all around it. (The house where the reception was, is beautiful. It's called Rose Lawn Museum. It's a Victorian mansion the renowned evangelist Sam Jones used to live in, in the late 1800s.) Thank goodness the caterer and baker were able to use the kitchen at Rose Lawn, and the trees were cleared literally just hours before the wedding, thanks to my sister staying on top of it. Everything turned out beautiful.

During the wedding, Pastor May, who had been with us through all the tragedies, was there to marry us, which was special. Terry sang "Keeper of the Stars" to me, and I don't think there was a dry eye in the church, including the pastors.

We had always said that we really didn't want kids, but if we ever changed our minds that we would talk about it. Well, about six years into our marriage, I started thinking about wanting a baby. When I started talking to Terry about it, he was feeling the same thing. So not much later, I was pregnant. I remember being so excited and so scared at the same time. I was so sick the entire time. By the end of the pregnancy, I had gone to the ER several times for fluids just from throwing up so much, and I only gained 14 pounds during the entire pregnancy. Of course, this is normal for a lot of pregnancies, but it's still hard.

As my due date approached, I started having contractions about five days before she was born. I'm a hairdresser, so I was doing hair until two days before I had her. I had gone to the doctor the morning before I had her, and everything was good, no high blood pressure, nothing; besides being sick, I was healthy the entire time. Well, that night, my contractions finally started coming every three-four minutes instead of the twenty minutes I had had all week. And then, as I got ready to head to the hospital, they went back to twenty minutes. I was so frustrated and tired. I decided to go to sleep and see what happened, which was okay, except the contractions were so strong they would wake me up, so finally I was like, "If I'm not going to have her then, I want them to stop!"

We headed to the hospital, and when I got there, they immediately admitted me, my blood pressure was high.

My Family

They started to induce labor, but I passed out; they wanted to try again, but I was like, no way! I did not want to pass out again from the drugs. Carmen's heartbeat started to slow down, so they ended up doing an emergency C-section. Once Carmen was born, the doctor said he was so thankful we ended up doing the C-section because her umbilical cord was so small and around her neck she would not have survived the delivery. Her umbilical cord was literally the size of a pencil. She was 5 lbs, 11 oz, and 19 inches long and healthy.

Later that night, one of the nurses that was on duty the night before came in and said, "I know you don't know me, but I know you through a mutual friend, and I know your faith in God. I don't think you realize it, but if you had not come in last night, your husband would have lost you and your daughter; your blood pressure was so high that you were at seizure level!" She was like, "God was totally protecting you!" And He was because I had no idea it was high; I was just tired of the pain from the contractions. It's your choice to look for the good or the bad; you are going to go through things, period! If you look for the good and where God is in the midst of it, it helps to get through it.

When Carmen was about four weeks old, I was in Bible study at church on a Wednesday night; I was so glad to be able to go and do and not be sick (even though she was worth every bit of the sickness). She was in her car seat when all of a sudden, she started choking! I grabbed her and flipped her over on her stomach and started patting her back to make whatever was stuck come up. We rushed her to Children's Healthcare in Atlanta. She was okay, but they couldn't figure out what happened, and the next day when I was in her doctor's office, she had the absolutely best nurse practitioner ever, Mr. Thomas. Once he realized how scared I was, he immediately put her on a heart monitor and figured out that she was choking because her milk was coming back up, but it wasn't making her throw it up. This happened several times daily; I had to flip her over and pat her back until it came up. It was very stressful. You already never sleep when you have a baby; add this on top, and I never slept.

I had a salon in my home, and my cousin was in getting her hair cut. I was telling her about Carmen, and she was like, "Girl, why haven't you got an anointed clothe on that baby!" I'm not sure why I had not. We had laid hands on her and prayed over her over and over. That night I had my mom pray over a cloth, and I immediately put it in her diaper bag because it was always near her. Acts 19:11–12 talks about Paul praying for the sick and them being healed. Even with the cloths he anointed, and people took to other people, they were getting healed and delivered. I grew up with a mom that would pray over the cloth. She'd say, "Remember, there's no power in it, it's just an outward step of faith." Once I did that, within a day, she never had any more spells from the choking! The Lord took that act of faith and healed her.

My Nephews

My two younger nephews, Christopher and Ryan, were such a big part of my life. Ryan belonged to Kevin, and Christopher to my sister Lisa. I loved these boys, and we did so much together. As a baby, Christopher would stay with my mom and me all the time. My sister's job required her to leave for work around six or six thirty in the morning to get there in time, so my nephew would spend the night, or my sister would bring him early in the morning. Either way, he came to our house asleep, she'd put him in bed with my mom, and we'd take care of him during the day. I absolutely loved it! I'd sing Christian songs to him while he drank his bottle, and as he got older, we would sit in the living room looking out the front window watching his "friends" play—his friends being the squirrels.

Ryan lived just a block away, and I'd go by and feed him his bottle sometimes. He used to have really bad reflux, and, one time, I was feeding and burping him, and the entire bottle came back up all over me! I knew I loved him when I didn't throw up. Unfortunately, my brother and his first wife got a divorce a few years after he was born, which changed the amount of time I saw him, but I still always stayed close and made sure I spent time with him. His mom was always good to let me come see him and get him.

The boys loved Terry when I started dating him. They were so excited we were getting married. I remember them getting into our limo at the wedding to ride with us to the reception and Christopher saying, "This is the best day of my life." It was so cute and made my heart happy!

We would take them on trips with us all the time. We took them on several cruises out west, to Dallas, Texas, to visit relatives, and Albuquerque, New Mexico, to Gatlinburg, Tennessee. Plus, we'd go to Six Flags and White Water all summer. I enjoyed being with them and doing for them. They were at my house all the time, or we would go get them to go eat. I spoiled them rotten while they were growing up and loved every minute of it. I tried to be the fun aunt.

It was Labor Day 2006, and all day long, I remember praying. I knew again something was wrong; I wasn't sure what. I remember driving up the hill on Old Mill Road in my town and telling my husband something wasn't right, to please pray with me, but that I didn't feel like it was my mom or us. I knew most of my family was at the lake drinking that day, so I was a little worried about that. I just couldn't put my finger on it, so I just prayed all day for protection for my entire family. Later that night, I had gotten in bed, and around 11:30, my phone rang. It was my ex-sister-law, Kevin's ex-wife. As soon as I saw the call. I grabbed it and said, "Please just tell me Ryan's okay!" She said he was but had been in an accident, and they couldn't get in touch with my brother. I, of course, headed over to him immediately. As soon as I got to him, I got out of the car and started crying, telling him I had been praying all day. I didn't know at the time whom for, but now I did!

He had just dropped off his girlfriend at the time and was heading back home when his tire went off the road, and his SUV rolled three times. He had to crawl out through the back window that was busted. He crawled through all of the glass and stuff everywhere. He walked away with glass in his leg, bruised up, and super sore muscles, but that was all. If his girlfriend had been in the car, it would have killed her because that entire side was caved in. It was a total miracle! If you had seen the car, it's amazing anyone survived. God just had His hand on him. Prayer does work!

Some Awesome Miracles

I grew up with a mom, who believed in the power of prayer and who knew how to reach the throne room of heaven! I am so thankful every day for her faith in the Lord and her leadership in teaching me to trust in God. It's the best gift she could have ever given me! She was my constant. Her relationship with the Lord is why I am like I am today. Her faith was so strong. As I said before, she would always say that when she got saved, she didn't just get saved, but that she fell in love with Jesus. And let me tell you, she lived that. She would lay on the floor for hours praying and reading her Bible. She loved to be used by the Lord, and it showed in her everyday life. She got the National Day of Prayer started in our hometown, and it's typically the largest one in Georgia. Her pastor, at her funeral, said that we as kids all had really big shoes to fill and that we probably would not be able to, and I agree with him. My mom was one of a kind.

I have a few stories to tell about how God moved.

The first is about a girl from our town. She was eleven years old when she had just gone into remission from cancer. We had been celebrating a few weeks before with her father about what God had done! While we were rejoicing, God gave me Proverbs 18:21, about how death and life are in the tongue, so be careful and guard what people speak over her. A few weeks later, she was at the Georgia Capital with her school, and she had proposed a mock bill for children with cancer. While there, she got really sick, and they took her to Children's Healthcare in Atlanta. Through testing, they found a different cancer that was not there at all three weeks before. This was on a Wednesday; by Friday, she wasn't doing good at all. I grabbed a stuffed bunny that had been Carmen's and had my mom pray over it and anoint it with oil. My mom literally prayed for over two hours for her, with the bunny believing in God for a miracle.

We weren't able to run it down Friday night, so we got up early Saturday and headed down. When we got there, she was not well, they had called the family in, and everything was shutting down. Her temperature was so high; they had her on ice. It was heartbreaking hearing her dad wailing in his best friends' arms. On the way down, the Lord gave me something to tell her dad. I first gave him the bunny and explained about an anointing cloth. Then shared with him what the Lord had given me: I told him if a bully was bullying his daughter at school, he wasn't going to go to the principal and tell her to do whatever their will was, but he was going to go after that bully and stop them. In this instance, the devil was bullying his daughter, and he needed to go after him in prayer! He took the bunny and laid it beside her in ICU. I didn't see him again. I had left the ICU waiting room to run to the restroom and saw her dad walking up and down a back hallway. He said, "I'm going after the bully in Jesus' name!" We had been there for a little over an hour, praying with people from our church. Before we left, her temperature had started coming down! I had someone call me later that day, and everything had stabilized so much that they were able to start chemo on her that night! She is now a young adult!

Another awesome story of God's grace and healing was a young man that had just graduated a month before from high school. He and his family were out boating and tubing in a lake near their home when another boat literally ran over him on the inner tube. He was life-flighted to Erlanger Hospital in Chattanooga, Tennessee. He was on life support, with swelling in the brain. He needed a miracle. Everyone in our community was praying for him. I knew who his mom was, but I did not know her. I felt led to take her an anointed cloth. I knew she would not know what it was. I asked the Lord, "If this is truly You, please open the door for me to even get into the hospital, and please let her accept what I am going to share with her." Well, as God always does, He opened the door. We were told how to get into the ICU waiting room through a back door, and as I came into the room, her dad saw me and immediately came over to me. I told him I had something to share with his daughter, and he took me to her. My heart broke. She looked up at me. Even though she never said a word, her eyes said, "I know you, but I'm not sure why you are here," but not in a bad way. Her dad walked over to her and said, "I know you don't know Tricia; you don't know all she has been through, but I do, so whatever she shares with you, please listen." I was so humbled and grateful for God opening the door for me to talk with her. I was only there a moment. I shared with her stories about Paul and believing in faith, the fact that the cloth had no power, it was just a step of faith, and if she didn't mind, asked to please put it near him or in his pillow. I truly don't know the timeline, but it wasn't too many days after his swelling went down and God absolutely showed up! He went on to college and graduated. The only thing was, he was having some seizures, but remember, the doctors didn't expect him to live. But God! But God had other plans!

Then there's Mike. Mike and his wife at the time went to our church. I did not know Mike at all. Our Sunday school class was asked to take up money and buy his family some food, because he had been in an accident. I volunteered to go buy the groceries and take them to their home, where his sister-in-law was staying with their seventeen-year-old son. See, Mike was riding his motorcycle, and someone ran a stop sign and hit him. He was life-flighted to Erlanger as well. He had swelling on the brain and was paralyzed from the chest down. The doctors really had no hope. When I took the groceries to his house, I also gave his sister-in-law an anointed cloth, again, telling her previous testimonies and how there was nothing in the cloth, that it was just a step of faith.

I kept up with everything going on every few weeks, and then one day, at church, this guy in a wheelchair came up to me and asked if I was Tricia Jordan, I was like, "Yes?" He said, "Well, I am Mike May." Oh, my goodness! I can't tell you how awesome it was to see him. Yes, he was still paralyzed, but he was alive and had no brain injuries. God, later, maybe even a year or more, gave me a word one morning for him about his healing and how He was going to heal him, but that man would not get glory for it. That same night, in a prayer meeting, he was attending when some young man came up and gave him the same word. Mike has not been totally healed yet, but God is slowly healing him.

God wants to heal you, God wants to set you free, God wants to deliver you, God wants to teach you to forgive! God loves you, He's a father. If you are a parent, what would you not do for your child or children?

The Arrest

My daughter, Carmen, is an actress. Labor Day, 2015, she had an audition in New York City, so we drove up. They ended up choosing her out of over 800 people; we were so excited. It was for a music video, and she was only twelve years old. When we were in LA in October, she went into the studio and laid the tracks down, and in November, we went back to New York to record the video for it. We were excited because our friends, who were missionaries in Costa Rica, were in town, and their two daughters were going to get to go with us. One had never been to the States, she was eighteen, and they had just adopted her from Costa Rica. The other one was fourteen.

The night before we were leaving for the quick trip, the bombing in Paris happened. It was a terrorist attack, and they had bombed a concert hall, a major stadium, and some restaurants. I always traveled with my gun except to New York. I knew their laws were strict, just like Chicago and California's; I didn't realize they were that different than theirs, though. I knew I couldn't carry one, that they did not honor my Georgia carry permit, but I thought I could have the gun locked and the bullets out away from it, just like in the other two states and when you fly. Well, because of the bombing the night before, I decided last minute to carry my gun with me. I knew I wasn't going to fight off any terrorists, but I just thought if anything did happen, at least I'd have it to help us hopefully get out of the city. I'm a Georgia girl, and after going through all I have been through, I believe in protecting myself.

I went through TSA in Atlanta with no issues. We got to New York, and everything went well. Carmen recorded her video; it was a song she wrote at twelve years old. It's called "You're Not Alone." The last night, we had a blast going to the Empire State Building, catching a ride on the taxi bicycles, and just cutting up in the streets. We got up early the next morning, heading to the airport. Once we got to La Guardia, I told the agent that I needed to check my gun, just like I do in every airport. She said, "Okay, no problem, just let me get security come to check you in." There was nothing abnormal about that. In several airports, they would come and walk me over to another counter to put my luggage through and then check it. So, I waited for about fifteen minutes, which was a little unusual. The two girls went ahead and checked in at the agent next to us, and I was getting a little antsy because I did not want to miss our flight. Next thing I know, the New York Port Authority was there, going through my bags and telling me they were going to be taking me with them. They were trying to find my bullets, which you can't have with your gun, so I had to hide them in my suitcase. I literally thought I was going to pass out. I called my husband and then my mom and asked her to please start praying, that they were going to keep me. Carmen was begging the lady to please let her go; she was so upset. She was never really without me too much. She was so scared, and so was I. I couldn't believe my baby was having to fly home without me. They sent Carmen home on the plane with our friends. Talk about you being caught off guard, but not God; He knew what was going to happen that Monday, November 16th, that I had no idea about, so He sent some sweet friends to be with my girl.

As she rounded the corner to go get on the plane, they handcuffed me; thank God they did not do it in front of her.

At the airport, I had to leave everything with my twelve-year-old, my wedding rings and my wallet, except my driver's license, credit card, and a hundred-dollar bill. I was pretty innocent; I never got into trouble, really, even as a kid. I was taken to the Port Authority and booked. I was a mess! I could not quit crying. I was so worried about her flying without me. I think I was more worried about her at that point than myself.

Once I was taken to the Port Authority, they booked me with a B-class felony; that's one step below a murderer. They then put me in a cell, and I was able to call Terry. I remember I had on new sweatpants I had literally just bought, and I had to cut the strings out of them. I was definitely scared and a little sick. I was always the girl who, if my mom told me not to go down a certain street, I didn't. Not even after I was grown. As they got ready to transport me to the jail in Queens, they handcuffed me again and were going to shackle me. I really felt like I was being arrested to prove a point, but once they actually arrested me, I felt like the lady felt like she made a mistake and regretted it. So at this point, when they went to shackle me, and I asked her not to, she didn't. Also, when they handcuffed me at the airport, I literally had marks on my hand when we got to the Port Authority, so she didn't put them on as tight this time. I think once they started checking, they could see I wasn't a threat or any problem. I was just broken. I cried so much.

Once at Queens, they took me to a holding cell. There was a young girl there; she was in her mid-20s. I wish I could remember her name. She was born in another country and was a singer/songwriter. She also struggled with alcoholism, which is why she was there that morning. At first, it was just us two, then, they started bringing more people in. I remember this sweet lady who worked there once came to ask me about someone representing me; I had no idea what she was talking about. She helped me with the questions, and then she said, "I can tell you are so upset. Is there anything I can do?" I then told her I was worried about my daughter and if she had gotten back to Georgia safely. She was so sweet, she took my husband's number and called to find out about her. She came back to me shortly and said she was okay, she was staying at the friend's house to hang with the girls until he got off of work, so she would have something to do to keep her busy. That helped me a lot, knowing Carmen was okay and safe.

As I was sitting there and these women kept coming into the cell, I remember telling the Lord that I wasn't Paul and Silas, I wasn't going to stand up in the middle of the cell proclaiming about Him, but that He obviously had me there, so to somehow please use me if He could. I know one reason He did. The young girl. I was able to love on her and talk to her about her life and what it was worth and about alcohol and how it destroys your life. I knew from experience because three of my brothers and sisters dealt with it, as did my uncles and my dad at one point. As she was being released after going before the judge, she gave me a big hug and cried. I really wish I had the wits about me to get her number, but I did not. There was also another lady, who was great; she was a black lady that kind of helped me through the day. She'd tell me what to expect next as they'd move us from different cells. She was really sweet to me; she kept saying, "I have been in here a lot, and you definitely don't need to be in here."

The Arrest

She was in there for hitting her neighbor, I think. Either way, she was great.

Everyone in the cell went before the judge but me. They put me with the evening judge because I was waiting on my attorney. My mom, who was as upset as I was, because I really never gave her any trouble growing up, had called my oldest brother for help. He had a friend from New York, who lived in Georgia, whom he called, and his friend then called a friend that was a head jailer in New York, who then called his friend, who was an attorney. They both showed up for me at the court hearing that evening. The head jailer was ready to pay my bail, which they had told him would be over $25,000. But, once we got into the courtroom, the judge took mercy on me and let me go without bail. I think the attorney also knew the judge from past occasions. I had to be back in January for my first court hearing. Once, I was outside of the courts and in the hallway, the gentlemen that had brought me money in case I needed it came out to tell me who he was. I was clueless. I didn't know any of this was going on. I just knew they delayed me seeing a judge because my brother had gotten me an attorney. I also remember seeing the jailer and hugging him and crying even though he was a complete stranger. He let me use his phone to book a plane trip home that night and to call my family. I grabbed a taxi out front and went immediately to the airport; I wanted to get home to my family as soon as possible. As I got to the airport and went through security, I was waiting on my plane, and of course, it was delayed. There were no payphones, so I finally got an employee from the airline to let me borrow her phone to call my husband to tell him it was delayed. I remember crying all the way home; I was so grateful to be going home. I was scared and alone. Once I landed, I remember waiting in baggage claim for Terry and Carmen; it was like 1:00 a.m. When I saw them, all I could do was hug them and cry; I'm not sure how I had any more tears; I had cried so much that day. I was just so glad to be home.

I was a total wreck, though; I couldn't eat or sleep for the next two months. Everything made me sick; my nerves were so shot. I had called the attorney in New York that came the night I was arrested to ask him what I needed to do. He, of course, wasn't too worried about my case. I remember feeling a lot of unease. Through just about everything I had been through in my life so far, no matter what, I always felt the peace of God, but this week I couldn't. I kept asking the Lord, "Why?" That through everything, even though I would be upset and go through human things, I typically still had peace. I remember finally getting to speak to him, and while I was on the phone with him, I felt the Holy Spirit nudge me to ask him how many of these cases he had handled. He said about three. I then knew that I had to find an attorney that was dealing with them daily.

We were on our way over to my mom's that night. When I got there, I got on my phone and started looking at attorneys in New York that dealt with gun arrests. There was one attorney's office that kept coming up; it was literally the only one out of the hundreds that should have. It was Tilem and Associates, PC. I called them first thing that Friday morning and told them everything. Within an hour, Peter Tilem called me back. I knew then he was the one whom I was supposed to be talking to. Then I had peace.

I had asked Peter what I needed to do to get out of this mess. We went over my story, and he then told me to get as many character reference letters as I could. I asked him how many, like a number, and he said as many as possible. I was like, "I'm from a small town in Georgia; I can get you as many as you need." He just said, "As many as you can." So, I prayed about it, and the Lord gave me about fifty names to reach out to. I kept the arrest quiet because I felt like the Lord gave me the Bible verse in Proverbs 18:21 about how death and life are in the power of the tongue. I didn't want anyone speaking over me that I was going to go to jail. Everyone I spoke with was wonderful. They immediately got their letters in within a week to Mr. Tilem's office. I had friends from then, childhood friends, attorneys that knew me, pastors, doctors, clients I had done for twenty-five-plus years, youth workers, state representatives, etc.... Once all of the letters got into his office, the office called and set up an interview with me to go over everything in my life, literally. This took about four hours. This was with Hillary Marr, who was then assigned to me as my attorney for the case. She was amazing and a God send! I remember her telling me that they typically couldn't get one or two letters in for months, but I had fifty come in, in one week! She said they were from every different walk of life, yet they all said the same thing about you. She said they never really meet people like me. So she was excited to talk with me and see who I was.

I was such a mess leading up to it. My fuse ran really short, I was snappy with everyone, and everything got on my nerves. I kept telling the Lord that I had always tried to be faithful to Him, to please show up for me on this.

As January 11, 2016, started to roll around, Hillary was trying to get everything done. This should have been the first court appearance of years; instead, the DA had offered a plea. If I pleaded guilty to disorderly conduct, I could get off with a misdemeanor instead of a B-class felony, which was one step below a murder, so of course, we took it, but I was still so upset, I just wanted it gone, I barely had speeding tickets, much let a misdemeanor on my record was horrible to me.

We drove up to New York, I was not at a place to fly again yet. We tried to make it as fun for Carmen as we could, so we spent the night in Washington, DC, and went to see some of the Smithsonians before driving to New York City. I kept praying for God to show up and work a miracle for me. On the way to New York, there was a double rainbow that literally ended in a church, and I remember telling my family that was my promise from God, that He had everything worked out.

We got to Queens that night, so I could be at the courthouse early the next morning. As I was waiting on Hillary to get there the next morning, I was nervous and sick, yet I still kept believing in God and praying for my miracle. I really wanted it to be wiped clean, God chose not to do that. When Hillary got there and went into the office to let them know we were there, the DA told her they were dropping it to a violation, that's just like a speeding ticket. So, it would stay on my record for six months as disorderly conduct and then drop off. I was so thankful and relieved. So, it went from a B-class felony to a violation, a total miracle!

We went before the judge, and as the DA told her that they had dropped it to a violation, she was like are you sure, and the DA proceeded to tell her why, I don't remember what she said. I was just thinking, let's get this hammer down so it's final. The judge hesitated and then finally slammed the hammer, and we were out! I had to pay a $350 fine for it all. Hillary was so excited. So we went from a B-class felony with a minimum of three to fifteen years in prison, with several years of court appearances, to a violation and no more court appearances. Tell me God doesn't show up. When He does, we act surprised, but we should just believe. It's just so hard to do, though; our human nature takes over. I was so overwhelmed with gratitude and so thankful I had listened to the Holy Spirit about the other attorney, even though I was very grateful for what he did do for me on the day of the arrest.

I waited until after five to call Hillary to let her know how much I really appreciated everything she had done. She was so sweet; she made me cry because she was like, "You said God had a purpose for this happening to you, and I am one of the purposes." I told my husband this was my $15,000 mission trip. You never know how you are going to affect someone's life, so always try to stay positive, even when it's extremely hard. You might just show them who Jesus is and help to change their lives.

In May, after my court case, John Stossel's assistant called and asked me to be on his show about my arrest in New York City, my attorney had given him my name, so my family and I went back to New York that June and I got to do my interview with him. I was excited about it, but it was also hard going back to the city again. I have since gotten over it and have been back several times. The interview has had over 17 million views so far. It was on his Facebook page as "Gun Owners Jailed" You never know what God is going to do if you are an open vessel.

The Hardest Thing
I Have Ever Been Through

Can you imagine me making that my chapter heading after everything else I have been through? Well, it's true. This chapter is about my mom.

My mom and I were really close, as I've stated before. I think the fact that it was just she and I when I was twelve made our relationship different, plus she was older when she had me, so the dynamics of her life were different than with my older brothers and sisters. My mom loved all of her children equally. Well, sometimes I felt like she loved my sister, Lisa, the most, but for real, she was extremely proud of her kids. She was always bragging on them and talking about them to everyone. We were her life.

Like I said, my mom and I had a little bit of a different bond. I think also, everything I had been through made me want to always be there to help and protect her. I never moved more than a mile or so from her. Especially as she got older. I wanted to be close by in case she needed me or my husband, which she did often. There were so many nights she would call, and we'd have to run over because she had fallen off of the bed or needed help with something.

My sister Lisa and her husband helped her. She kept their son, which was wonderful for me because we became so close, so my sister would bring her dinner, and her husband would cut her grass. It was such a blessing for her.

My brother Thomas wasn't around much, unfortunately he dealt with alcoholism. Even though he was very successful with money, he had been dealing with alcoholism since he was in his teens. Anyway, as he got older, he started paying to have my mom's grass cut and have someone clean her house.

My sister Linda did stuff for my mom too, but she lived further away and traveled all over the world with her job, and had been raising her grandson. But if mom needed to go to a doctor's visit I couldn't take her to, or she found out she needed to go to a doctor, she'd research and take her. My mom also loved to stay at her house and sit out on her front porch.

My brother Kevin used to work on cars in my mom's garage at the lower driveway of her home. If she absolutely needed him, he would come. He was her baby boy. She'd say he may be six feet four inches, but he's still "my baby boy." She used to also say when he was younger, he was her praying partner. He is the awesome mechanic of the family, so he kept her car running.

Then there was my mom and I. As I said before, I never wanted to be too far from her. As she got older and couldn't drive anymore, I would take her to most of her doctor's visits, to the grocery store, or get them for her. I would take her to church, even when we were going to a different church than her; I'd go take Carmen to our church on Wednesday nights and go pick up my mom and take her to her church because I knew she loved it and needed it. Then, I'd go get Carmen from our church and run back and pick my mom up from her church and take her home.

The Hardest Thing I Have Ever Been Through

It was tiring but worth it. My mom would go on most of my trips, not all, but a good bit of them with me. She loved Carmen, as she did all of her grandkids, but I tried really hard to make it so that she could just enjoy her and not have to help me raise her. She helped raise the other grandchild and thank the Lord she could. How awesome to have a grandmother be able to help, especially her with her love of the Lord.

My mom's health was already declining a little bit when I got arrested; it really upset her, so I'm sure it didn't help her much. Then, on October 19, 2016, my mom fell. I was at Disney, which we loved to go to with Carmen. Thomas had started going by to see her with his dog, which she absolutely loved since he had never come by too much. He was retired and finally decided to make time to. He was with her that late afternoon when she thought she heard someone knock at the kitchen door, so she got up to see, but no one was there. I still haven't figured out why he let her go to the door instead of him getting up to go for her. I would have jumped up instead. Anyway, on her way back into the den at her house, she fell over her rug, she lived by herself and was always so careful, so it never made sense to me how she did this, but she did and broke her shoulder. Well, when you are eighty-six and fall and have a break, unless the good Lord does something, you don't usually recoup too well. My mom was in the hospital, and for the first time in my life, I did not run back home. My year had been so stressful from my arrest, and this was my family getaway that was so desperately needed, so we spent a few more days at Disney, which I should have never done. I knew she was going to be at the hospital, and her orthopedic doctor was a client and friend of mine, so I had called him, but he was out of town, so I then called someone else in his practice whom we went to church with, and I booked their trips (I also own a small travel agency). He went and took care of my mom. She had to stay in the hospital for a little bit, then they transferred her to rehab, but he knew she would have to have surgery. My mom's health was so good that at eighty-six, he was able to give her a full shoulder replacement. Not very many people would be able to do that at her age. At rehab, I would go every morning and get her dressed, help her eat, help her get on the potty, you name it, and I had someone with her all the time. I couldn't stand to think of her being by herself; she was getting a little confused from all of the meds. My mom barely took an Advil for pain, and doctors at the hospital where she was had put her on extremely high doses of pain medicine. She and I reacted to medicine alike, and I couldn't take the medicines they had her on, but because I wasn't there when she fell and my brother was, he felt like he knew best. I understand he loved her like I did, but he still did not have the same relationship or knowledge that I did. But my brother has money and loves to take charge. Unfortunately, my sisters and I had a falling out about a month before this. Lisa had told Linda that I had my mom change her will and put me on it with my middle sister instead of her. I truly don't remember doing that. I remember my mom being worried years before that, with Linda traveling all over the world and with Lisa and I doing everything mostly for her anyway that she wanted to add me instead. If it was different than that, I don't remember. Either way, it didn't matter, except that they convinced my mom to change it and had her lie to me, which is not something my mom would typically do. I truthfully didn't care, except I was the one who took care of her the most, so I needed medical power, and the fact that they did it being sneaky made it weird because I had one on my feelings that morning. Lisa offered to take my mom to a doctor's appointment, which almost never happened, and I could always use the help; plus, my mom was excited she was taking her. When I got up that morning, I knew something wasn't right. I called my mom to check on her, and she was already gone with my sister. Well, her appointment wasn't until later that day, and I knew my mom didn't feel like going places, so I called her. When she answered, I asked her where she was, and she said Belk, and then the Holy Spirit said, "No, she's at a lawyer's office," so I asked her, and she said she was, that my sister had told her to tell me she was at Belk. Well, I'm going to tell you that I wish more than anything that I had not said a word to her about her will after that, especially since she fell and since everything I had to go through with my family. The only reason I was really concerned was because Lisa was dealing with alcoholism at the time, and I wanted to make sure my mom was going to be taken care of. Now, my sister, before alcoholism, would have done everything for my mom, but that disease is a monster. So, this happened and my mom went back and redid her will again and then a few weeks later she fell. Man, that's when all hell broke loose. Everyone, including me, felt like we knew what was best for our mom. If it had just been my sisters and I, we could have probably worked through it, but my older brother being involved really made it hard. He was never around, so he knew very little about my mom. Of course, he didn't want her hurting, and he had done drugs before, so he could handle a lot of pain meds; my mom could not, so he wanted to keep her drugged so she wouldn't hurt, and I wanted to get her well, which she couldn't function on the pain meds. My sisters, unfortunately, especially my oldest sister, took his side, and they hated each other my entire life, so I was so surprised. I was really struggling because she was siding with all three of my siblings, who were all struggling with alcoholism at the time. Well, things got worse. My mom had her surgery, and in the process, they all turned on me. So, I was pretty much left to take care of her on my own. Thomas would come by, but he had started so much of this mess.

I then made things worse when I brought her home. I needed help and had rented out her apartment in her basement to a lady from my church who supposedly knew how to help take care of elderly people. She was still renting out my mom's basement, and I was paying her to come upstairs and pretty much live and help me. I had a thirteen-year-old, I was home-schooling, I was a hair-dresser, and I ran a travel agency. I was trying so hard not to use much of my mom's money because that was some of our issues. My brother had money, so to spend my mom's little bit wasn't anything for him, but I knew I had to preserve as much as possible. She was so confused all the time after her surgery and really struggling, and they would come in and sit down and tell her that she had enough money to stay in her house for four years; you don't do that to someone who has the beginning stages of dementia, so she was in constant turmoil every day. Everything had changed, she was no longer independent. She could no longer use her right arm, she had to have help and someone around all the time, and then they kept this mess up, I finally couldn't handle it any longer, so I was like, let me have total power of attorney or let them, I just can't do this any longer. So, she signed it over to me, and then she wanted to change her will again. I really didn't care; my mom didn't have anything. The only thing she had that I was supposed to get was her house, and Carmen was supposed to get the diamond ring my dad gave her

The Hardest Thing I Have Ever Been Through

for their 25th anniversary. I had told her for years that if they fought me for anything they could have it, it was just material things, the only thing I cared about was taking care of her, and I meant it.

Well, unfortunately, the lady I had hired to help and live in her basement was a pro at getting into families that had issues like ours and helped put gasoline on the fire, and boy, did she. I was so stupid, the Holy Spirit kept telling me she was no good, but I was so desperate for help I did not listen to Him, and I made a mess out of everything.

In May 2017, my brothers and sisters sat down with my mom and convinced her to sign power of attorney over to my oldest brother, which she would have never done, but they told her it was to help me. Little did she know, it was not at all. My family accused me of using my mom's money, which I did not. She had around $90,000 when I became her power of attorney in December 2016, I had spent around $8,000, $4,000, which was for a new air conditioner unit, and the other $4,000 was for the help I was paying. I did everything I could for myself to keep from using her money because I knew that it was supposed to take care of her needs to be, and then what was left over was supposed to go to my younger brother. In the process, I was putting myself and my family in a financial issue because I wasn't working enough. My husband started working two jobs to try to make up the difference. They also accused me of elderly abuse, which broke my heart. I would *never* hurt my mom. Everyone knew that. And when my oldest brother tried to accuse me of that at the hospital, the doctor told him there were no signs of it, and then the nurse actually came back to me and said that if anyone knew me, they knew better. She also said that he had caused issues there before. My mom's surgeon had also said my brother wasn't allowed back in his office right after her surgery. When they had her sign it, I had people from all over call me and offer to testify if I took them to court. I had doctors, attorneys, pharmacists, pastors, friends, and tons of people. But I knew that if I did, it would only hurt my mom because she was heading toward her last days, and they would not be there. It was the hardest thing I have ever been through in my life; she really didn't understand what she was doing; she just thought she was helping me to help her. It broke me more than anything. I lay in bed and cried for over a week; I couldn't function. I couldn't quit crying. I would cry, pray, read my Bible, and lay in a fetal position. I listened to Mercy Me's "Even If" and Kari Jobe's "I Am Not Alone" over and over. I knew I needed to fill my spirit with as much of who God is as I could because I could not do this myself. I was so hurt, lonely, and totally devasted. I couldn't eat, and I couldn't work. Nothing. I lost my mom and my family during this time in my life.

During that week, the Lord gave me, in my devotion one day, the story of Joseph and his brothers and how they were jealous of his relationship with his dad. I'm not sure if my family was or not, but the Lord gave that to me three times that week. It was in my devotion first, then in my Bible reading, and then in an email that I got weekly with little lessons in them. It was Genesis 37. Not being able to take care of my mom was the worst thing ever. I couldn't do anything for her. Can you imagine doing almost everything for her and then, you no longer can. I remember they had to take her to the hospital, and they had to call me to find out what she was allergic to because they didn't know. She'd call me and ask me to go take her somewhere or go do something for her, and I couldn't.

The Hardest Thing I Have Ever Been Through

When they had her sign that over to him, I took everything of hers and left it at her house. Her checkbook, bank account info, all the receipts, and her jewelry. Because she had health care workers in her home, I had brought it and put it in my closet to protect it. I wish I had taken it to my sisters, but thought they would get it, but they didn't so most of it was gone. I had changed her two life insurance policies over to my husband and me because my middle sister was supposed to get them, which I didn't mind, I just didn't want to be stuck with a bunch of bills or my mom needing help or no money to bury her with, since she wasn't helping me at the time. My intentions were not bad at any time. And if you knew me, you should have known that. Anything that I would not have needed for my mom would have gone to Lisa. That was what my mom wanted, just like my youngest brother; whatever money I had used of my mom's that was supposed to be his inherence to take care of her. My husband and I were going to give to him by taking a loan out or once we sold our house and moved into hers, since I was supposed to get it. I'm sure, though, if you are being fed a bunch of lies and you are already against each other, you would start to believe them. I really thought once my family saw I wasn't spending my mom's money, they would stop and see what was going on, but they didn't. The last year of my mom's life was hell. She ended up in an assisted living home, which was nice, but she always wanted to be in her home. The lady that was renting the basement and helping me with my mom, I had always made her pay rent so I could evict her at any time, but when Thomas took over, he kept paying her, and she no longer had to pay rent, so they couldn't just get her out of my mom's house, which is one reason she had to go into the assisted living. My husband's car was giving us fits while I was taking care of my mom, so I sold it and drove my mom's car. I had been driving it to take her to the doctor, buy her groceries, pick up her meds, etc... I worked from home, so I didn't use it much. He made me return it the week he took over, and he told me he would have me arrested if I didn't. So, the lady living at my mom's house drove it instead. She had a car. I can promise you my mom didn't mind me driving it. But of course, Thomas lied to her about that too. He was horrible to me; he would call and leave horrible voicemails, threatening me and saying horrible things to me. His phone calls and threats finally got so bad I had to tell Linda if he continued, I was going to turn him in to the cops for terroristic threats. Unfortunately, what he accused me of, he did to my mom, he went through the little bit of money she had. I really don't care about the money or the fact that they changed the will; all I cared about was taking care of her and the fact that they lied about me and turned people I love against me. I guess those people didn't know me too well because if they did, they should have known better than to believe the people in my mom's life who were dealing with alcoholism. They stole the last year of my mom's life from me.

Because I was hurting so much and was suffering from my family so badly, I just wanted to run and get as far from the hurt as I could, so my husband and I decided to move to California with our daughter to help further her career as an actress. We put our house on the market and got a contract for May 24, 2017; it had been a year since they had her sign the papers. I wasn't telling her I was moving to California because she would not have understood, especially with her dementia, so I was just going to tell her I'd be out there for five or six weeks, then I was going to come home for a week and do my clients hair and see her. We used to go out for stuff with Carmen all the time, so I thought she'd understand that. I just didn't want to add to anything with the dementia. I went to see her Sunday night, May 20th. She was a little mad at me at first because they had changed her room, and I wasn't able to call her and talk with her. I had tried several times over the last few days, but they never took the phone to her; once I got there, though, she got okay and was glad to see me. I took her down for dinner, and she ate well, then offered me her cake. I said, "Mom, I think you will want it; it's chocolate," and she was funny; she said, "Oh, yes, I do!"

I then took her back to her room. They had a family friend staying with her; she was a caregiver and was wonderful.

Right as I got home, Joan called to have me come back and said she couldn't get in touch with my sisters and my mom had had a spell. So, I headed back; they had moved her about thirty minutes from my house. It was the first time in my entire life that she had not been a mile or two from me. I was almost there when she called and said they got her to sleep, not to come. I later found out Linda told her to not let me come. I worked that Monday since I was getting ready to move to California that Thursday. Then, on Tuesday, while I was at work, the assisted living called me and said my mom had had a spell and that I needed to get there. So I finished up on my client what I had to; she had color on her and then headed to my mom. I was so confused because on Sunday, she was fine, and even with the spell, they acted like she was okay. When I got there, she was totally unresponsive; I was so upset. I really didn't understand, and I didn't understand why they weren't taking her to the hospital, and then I found out they had called in hospice months before. I had to go back to work, remember, I couldn't do anything anyway, so I told her

I loved her and that I would be back. I went back that night and stayed with her and my older sister. She would stabilize when I came in the room. So, all night she held my hand, and I laid with her most of the night, and she was stable. Once I left the next morning, I had so much to do to get out of my house, and I still had clients to do, so I was working when they called and said she wasn't going to make it, to please get there. I left with my emergency flashes on and took off. They had asked me to pull up to the front door, and they would park my car. When I got there, my two sisters and my oldest brother were there, but not Kevin, he was never there. Once I got there, I told her to go be with Jesus and my dad. That's what she had lived her whole life for, it was to see Jesus, but of course, she stabilized some again, so then my family started leaving, they had other things to do, and it was just my oldest sister and I again. I loved on her; I told her I was going to be okay and that she was good to go. She was ready, especially spiritually, if anyone was, she was. I finally left my sister with her because I really felt like if I was there, she wasn't going to go on, which seemed about right; she passed a few hours later. I couldn't believe my mom was gone. I no longer had a mom or dad on this earth, and really no brothers or sisters. This was the time I should have been able to cry in their arms; instead, I had to do it alone, except for my husband and daughter, and thank God for the good friends.

She had put in her will that she wanted me to plan her funeral, so I had to make sure through the assisted living that my brother would pay for it out of what was left of her estate, and he told them he would, so I called the funeral home and had them pick her up. I met my middle sister that next morning to pick out her casket and plan it all since I had no idea what kind of money I could spend. I then went back at two and did her hair and make-up, which was nice that I was able to have that last time with her, even though her spirit wasn't there. It was good for me, and I was glad to be able to do her hair for the last time.

I then left, went to my closing on my home, went by our house and picked up Carmen and our dogs, and headed to the hotel to check in, I wish I had asked to stay in the house that night, but I wasn't in any mind frame to do that, so I was late to my mom's viewing. We had to have everything quick because her pastor was leaving that Saturday for a mission trip, so we had her viewing that night and her funeral at two that next day, which was Friday.

Her funeral was great; you could feel God's presence so strong, I just worshiped. For months, when I would hear the song by Chris Tomlin, "Home," on the radio, I would cry and pray I could have it played at her funeral. It was my mom to a T, and look, God worked that out for me, and I was able to have it played. My Husband sang at her funeral; she loved to hear him sing. One of the songs that my mom would listen to over and over all day when I was growing up on her record player was "Jesus, Just the Mention of Your Name," so he sang that and "Go Rest High" She loved that song as well. Her pastor Jacob King preached her service, and I remember him saying that we, as her children, had big shoes to fill and would probably never be able to due to her walk with the Lord. I agree with him. My mom was one of a kind, and her faith was one of a kind.

We went to the graveside; then, I went to meet my friend and her daughter to say goodbye before we left town. If it wasn't for Judy, I would not have made it through the almost two years of hell with my mom and family. God sent her and her daughter to Carmen and me when I needed them most. I then went back to my mom and dad's grave and Tracey and Tyra and Destiny's. Then, picked up my cats and left Cartersville forever.

You want to talk about God being in control. I was so torn about leaving my mom to move to California, but with everything that had happened, we had prayed and felt like we should. When my mom passed the day before I was moving unexpectedly, I felt like God was telling me He had set it all up and to see He was in control. See, I never would have moved to California if I was taking care of my mom, so in the end, my family really did me a favor because my move there was one of the best things I ever did.

That was probably one of the hardest drives I have ever made. I cried all the way, I couldn't believe she was gone, and I was so mad at my family; I hated them, I mean, *hated* them. I had to pray every day and ask the Lord to help me love them and to ask for forgiveness for hating them so much. I know we were all to blame; it wasn't just them or just me, it was all of us, but what they did to my mom and me the last year of her life was taking a lot for me to forgive them. I'd sit in church and cry because I really wanted to pray that my brother Thomas would die and knew that I had to forgive him instead. So, every day I asked for forgiveness for my hate, and every day I asked the Lord to help me love and forgive them. And guess what? One day, I no longer wanted my brother to die, and I was able to start praying for him. It was slow at first, but this is what my mom wanted because, at the end of the day, the thing my mom wanted most was to have all of her children in heaven with her and my dad. And finally, one day, I was just able to forgive them. I still don't have a lot of contact with my family, only a little with my two sisters and none with my brothers, but I can honestly pray for them without hate. Though it took a lot of prayers, the one thing I do feel like is you have to forgive and learn to love again, but you don't have to have them in your life. God gave me peace with that, so I pray that they have a relationship with the Lord and that one day they can forgive me too. I know more than anything that my mom wants them in heaven with her. That was her prayer daily, to have all of her kids with her in heaven.

KNOWING GOD

I have other stories I could share, but most importantly, I hope and pray that if you are not a Christian or that if you have prayed the sinners' prayer but don't have a daily walk with the Lord, everything I have been through will help you know that you can have a daily walk of total dependence on Him. He is there for you, no matter what. We still go through things; we have pain, we cry, we mourn, and we hurt (emotionally and physically), but the difference is knowing Him on a personal level to help you get through it all. God is the only way I could have made it through everything I have been through. Even when your world is upside down, He will give you peace and help you through it. He loves you so much that He sent His only Son to die for your sins to save you and give you peace, to be there for you. You are going to go through things, period, as a Christian or as a sinner, but going through it with His presence in your life is what matters most. My husband one time sang at a three-year-old's funeral that died of meningitis. He said, "Tricia, you could tell they didn't have a personal relationship with the Lord." He said it was awful, the parents not having any hope of seeing their baby again.

Don't you want hope? Peace that passes all understanding and love? That's what Christ has to offer you. He wants to be there for you through the good and the bad. He wants you to know that even when it's awful, even when the flames are burring, He's still there helping you, holding you. My favorite poem growing up was "Footprints in the Sand." The last verse was:

"You promised me Lord, that if I followed you, you would walk with me always. But I have noticed that during the most trying periods of my life there has only been one set of footprints in the sand. Why, when I needed you most, have you not been there for me?"

The Lord replied, "The years when you have seen only one set of footprints, my child, is when I carried you."

This is what you want from the Lord; you want to know that He's the one carrying you, holding you, and giving you peace even when you shouldn't have it. God made you do the one thing He cannot do, and that is to worship Him, and what you get from worshipping Him is more than what He gets from us.

I pray if you don't know Christ, you ask Him into your heart to guide you, so He can show you who He is, and if you do know Him, that you get in your Bible and grow your daily walk with Him. Let God show you who He really is. I love to listen to Christian music daily to help my spirit stay focused on who Christ is; it's so encouraging. My favorite song right now is "Give Me Jesus" by Upper Room.

Knowing God

Know you are loved; God loves you more than anything and anyone.

I pray God's blessing on you, may His peace rest on you, in Jesus' name!

—Tricia Jordan

"I can do all things through Christ who strengthens me!"

Phillippians 4:13

My mom and dad in 1969

Myself and Tyra

My dad and I (I loved drinking out of the hose from him)

My mom and I

My dad and I in our kitchen

Bo from Beaumont, Tx. I had to have a walker like hers.

Me with our tinsel Christmas tree

My dad with his dog Shane

My monkey I got from Santa

Tracy, Tyra and myself

Myself, Tracy and Tyra

**My mom, myself and Aunt Dru in
Old Town Albuquerque at The La Hacienda**

My Aunt Dru, Uncle Grady, my dad and mom and myself

My mom and dad in front of our fireplace at my home

My mom and Carmen

Terry, Carmen, and myself

Printed in the USA
CPSIA information can be obtained
at www.ICGtesting.com
JSHW011756250924
70442JS00009B/45